PAMPHLETS ON AMERICAN WRITERS · NUMBER 6

UNIVERSITY OF MINNESOTA

Thomas Wolfe

BY C. HUGH HOLMAN

UNIVERSITY OF MINNESOTA PRESS · MINNEAPOLIS

Printed in the United States of America at
the North Central Publishing Company, St. Paul

◆ 3

Library of Congress Catalog Card Number: 60-62857

third printing 1963

Distributed to high schools in the United Stattes by
McGraw-Hill Book Company, Inc.
New York   Chicago   Corte Madera, Calif.   Dallas

PUBLISHED IN GREAT BRITAIN, INDIA, AND PAKISTAN BY THE OXFORD
UNIVERSITY PRESS, LONDON, BOMBAY, AND KARACHI, AND IN
CANADA BY THOMAS ALLEN, LTD., TORONTO

THOMAS WOLFE

C. HUGH HOLMAN is Kenan professor of English and the chairman of the department at the University of North Carolina. He is a co-author of *The Development of American Literary Criticism* and of the revised edition of *A Handbook to Literature.*

⤴ *Thomas Wolfe*

THOMAS WOLFE grappled in frustrated and demonic fury with what he called "the strange and bitter miracle of life," a miracle which he saw in patterns of opposites. The elements of life and of art seem to have existed for him as a congeries of contradictions, and he could not understand a thing until its negation had been brought forth. The setting down of these opposites is the most obvious single characteristic of his work, the significant parts of which are four vast novels, two collections of short stories, and an essay in criticism — all fragments of an incomplete whole, only the most shadowy outlines of which are discernible.

Even the titles of his books — *Look Homeward, Angel,* with its suggestion of near and far; *Of Time and the River; From Death to Morning; The Web and the Rock; You Can't Go Home Again,* with its idea of home and exile; *The Hills Beyond,* with its suggestion of movement, of extension — reflect this view of experience. So do his geographical oppositions — South and North, country and city, plain and "enfabled rock," America and Europe — and the contrasting pairs into which he regularly grouped his characters — father and mother, Jew and Gentile, South and North Carolinian, poor and rich, true artist and aesthete. Wolfe's vision of himself carried the same pattern of oppositions; in *The Web and the Rock* Esther Jack sums up the autobiographical hero with these words: "He has the face of a demented angel . . . and there is madness and darkness and evil in his brain. He is more cruel than death, and more lovely than a flower. His heart was made for love, and it is full of hate and darkness."

There is also a basic conflict of themes in Wolfe's work. He declared, "I have at last discovered my own America. . . . And I shall wreak out my vision of this life, this way, this world and this America, to the top of my bent, to the height of my ability, but with an unswerving devotion, integrity and purity of purpose." He saw himself as one with Walt Whitman, Mark Twain, and Sherwood Anderson, whom he called "men who have seen America with a poet's vision." The "epic impulse," the desire to define in fiction the American character and to typify the American experience, was obsessively present in his work. Yet another theme, contradictory but equally persistent in his work, was loneliness and the isolation of the incommunicable self. In a major sense, his subject matter was himself, his self-discovery and his groping toward self-knowledge; his forte was the lyrical expression of personal emotion and the rhetorical expression of personal attitudes. Aside from Whitman, no other American writer ever celebrated himself at such length, with such intensity, or with so great a sense of his own importance as Wolfe did. The private self and the public seer were roles that he was never quite able to harmonize, and yet he persisted in playing them both.

This fundamental concern with opposites is reflected in Wolfe's literary style itself — in the balanced antitheses that abound in his writing, in his shocking juxtaposition of images, in his use of contradictory phrases, such as "changeless change." In fact, Wolfe was a writer with two distinctive and contrasting styles. On one level he wrought with lyrical intensity a web of sensuous images capable of evoking from his readers a response almost as intense as that resulting from direct experience. Of American writers in this century, Ernest Hemingway is Wolfe's only equal at the evocative representation of the physical world through images so startlingly direct that they seem to rub against the reader's raw nerve ends. Wolfe said, "The quality of my memory is characterized, I believe, in a more than ordinary degree by the intensity of its sense impressions, its power to evoke and bring back the odors, sounds, colors, shapes, and feel of things with concrete vividness." At its best his style was superbly suited for transferring this concrete vividness to the reader.

Yet Wolfe was seldom content to let the scene or the senses speak for themselves; rather, he felt an obligation to define the emotion which he associated with the scene and to suggest a meaning, a universality, a significance through rhetorical exhortation. The resulting passages are marked by extravagant verbal pyrotechnics — by apostrophe, by incantation, by exhortation, by rhapsodic assertion, and, all too often, by rant and bombast. The lyric style evokes in the reader the ineffable emotion called forth in Wolfe by the scene; then the rhetorical assertion attempts to utter the ineffable and to articulate the transcendent aspects of the scene which Wolfe fears that the reader otherwise may miss. While passages in this second style often succeed magnificently in lifting the reader with their cadenced chants to glimpse Wolfe's ultimate visions, it is also true that such passages sometimes degenerate into dithyrambic incantations that become strident, false, and meaningless. Few writers have been so clearly at the same time both the masters and the slaves of language.

The same contrasts are apparent in the structural qualities of Wolfe's fiction. On the level of dramatic scene, fully realized and impacted with immediacy, Wolfe could construct magnificently. Single episodes of his work, published separately as short stories, are powerful narrative units. "The Child by Tiger," first a short story in the *Saturday Evening Post* and later an episode in *The Web and the Rock*, is a clear example; so are "Only the Dead Know Brooklyn," "The Lost Boy," and "An Angel on the Porch." In the middle length of the short novel he worked with perhaps his greatest effectiveness. *The Web of Earth* — in a structural sense, his most completely successful piece of work — *The Portrait of Bascom Hawke* (later fragmented and distributed through *Of Time and the River* as a portrait of Bascom Pentland), and *The Party at Jack's* (incorporated in *You Can't Go Home Again*) represent strong dramatic and narrative writing, rich in subject matter, firm in control, objective in point of view.

Furthermore, Wolfe projected ambitious plans for his books. Out of the experiences which were to be the material of his fiction he wished to weave a myth of his native land, an embodiment of its nature and its spirit. At a time when the American critic was just beginning to be concerned with the newer concepts of myth, Wolfe wrote, in the manuscript later published as the title piece of *The Hills Beyond*: "The Myth is founded on *extorted* fact; wrenched from the context of ten thousand days. . . . For it is not a question of having faith, or lack of it. It is a simple fact of seeing." In order to contain and define this mythic aspect of human experience, Wolfe sought in old myths and in fable, as well as in the structure of his own experience, the enclosing form for his utterance. *Of Time and the River* in one of its earlier projections was to be called *Antaeus*, and its characters were to symbolize Heracles, Poseidon, Gaea, Helen, Demeter, Kronos, Rhea, Orestes, Faustus, Telemachus, Jason. After outlining the proposed plot in a letter to Maxwell E. Perkins, his editor, he wrote: "Now, don't get alarmed at all this and think I'm writing a Greek myth. All of this is never mentioned once the story gets under way, but . . . it gives the most magnificent plot and unity to my book." Such projects are one of the staples of Wolfe's correspondence with the editors at Scribner's and at Harper's and with his agent.

Yet, in sharp contrast to the dramatic power in individual scenes and the magnificent and mythic scope in plan, the realized larger units of his work show a formlessness and plotlessness that have baffled and perplexed the critic of Wolfe since he first pub-

8

lished a novel. The structure of his works, at least on the surface, seems to be the simple chronological pattern of his own life, their incidents those participated in or witnessed. Scholars and critics have explored the close relationship of Wolfe's work to his life, and they have found that, despite his frequent disclaimers that his work is no more autobiographical than that of other novelists, the use of direct experience and the representation of actual persons and events are very great in his novels. Floyd C. Watkins, who examined Wolfe's use of materials drawn from his home town, Asheville, concluded, "there are many more than 300 characters and places mentioned by name or described in *Look Homeward, Angel,* and probably there is not an entirely fictitious person, place, or incident in the whole novel." Wolfe's disarming statement, "Dr. Johnson remarked that a man would turn over half a library to make a single book: in the same way, a novelist may turn over half the people in a town to make a single figure in his novel," is no defense at all when the people of the town are merely represented under the thinnest and most transparent disguises, and when the changes in name are as slight as "Chapel Hill" to "Pulpit Hill," "Raleigh" to "Sydney," "Woodfin Street" to "Woodson Street," or "Reuben Rawls" to "Ralph Rolls." His father's name is changed from "W. O. Wolfe" to "W. O. Gant," his mother's from "Eliza Westall Wolfe" to "Eliza Pentland Gant," his brother's from "Ben Wolfe" to "Ben Gant."

Wolfe's artistic method was a combination of realistic representation and romantic declaration; and it seems to have reflected accurately a contradictory — or perhaps double — view of the nature of art. On one hand, he was committed to the detailed, exact, accurate picturing of the actual world — committed to such an extent that he found it hard to represent anything that he had not personally experienced. On the other hand, his view of the nature and function of art was essentially that of the nineteenth-century Romantic poets and critics.

In one sense this aesthetic view was a natural outgrowth of his education. Five teachers had major influences on Wolfe, and four of them were clear-cut romantics. Margaret Roberts, who taught him for four years in a boys' preparatory school, made an indelible impression upon him with her love for the English poets; Mrs. Roberts, represented in *Look Homeward, Angel* as Margaret Leonard, filled the boy with a corresponding love of Wordsworth, Burns, Coleridge, Herrick, Carew, Jonson, Shakespeare, Poe, Hawthorne, Melville, and Scott. At the University of North Carolina he studied under Horace Williams, a philosophy professor whom he represented as Vergil Weldon and whom he called "Hegel in the Cotton Belt." Williams, who was a mystic, taught him a rather loose form of the Hegelian dialectic, in which a concept, or thesis, inevitably generates its opposite, or antithesis, and the interaction of the two produces a new concept, or synthesis. He also studied under Frederick Koch, who was beginning his work with the Carolina Playmakers and was encouraging his students to write folk plays, finding and underscoring the strange in the commonplace. Wolfe's first successful literary efforts were one-act plays written for Koch and produced by the Playmakers with Wolfe acting in them. At Harvard an important influence was John Livingston Lowes, who was writing *The Road to Xanadu* while Wolfe was a graduate student in his classes and whose view of the nature of Coleridge's imagination remained for Wolfe until his death a truthful picture of the workings of the artist's mind. At Harvard, too, he was influenced by George Pierce Baker, famous as the director of the "47 Workshop" in drama, although he later broke with Baker, at least partially as a result of dissatisfaction with the brittle and essentially anti-romantic views of students whom Baker applauded.

The marked romanticism of his aesethetic theory, with its pronounced distrust of almost all forms of intellectualism and its emphasis on the expression of the artist's feelings as the highest objective of a work of art, was at a polar extreme from the view Wolfe later developed of the novelist as national prophet obligated to represent the social scene; and his own novels are caught between the tug of the representation of the nation and the expression of the self.

Wolfe's tendency to see and to express things in terms of oppositions may have been learned at the feet of Horace Williams; it is possible that, as some critics have asserted, it represented a failure of his mind adequately to grapple with the problems before it; certainly it was, to some extent, an expression of his southern qualities, for the typical native of the southern states is fascinated by paradox, enamored of ambiguity, devoted to the particular and the concrete, and, although a dreamer of grandiose dreams, seldom the articulator of effective larger structures. The men of Wolfe's region were, like Wolfe himself, caught between the romantic view of their own past and the realistic fact of their present poverty. And over the years they have proved themselves capable of living with unresolved contradictions. Yet Thomas Wolfe was marked almost from his birth by certain unique paradoxes, which formed a peculiar aspect of his life, and therefore an inevitable aspect of his autobiographic art.

Thomas Wolfe was born in Asheville, North Carolina, which he was to call Altamont and Lybia Hill in his novels, on October 3, 1900. He was, therefore, a southerner, yet his native state in 1900 was in the midst of its espousal of the Populist movement that has left a heritage of liberalism in educational, social, and economic matters quite different from that in most of the rest of the South. Furthermore, Wolfe came from a mountain town far removed from even the dream of a South of tall white columns and banjo-strumming darkies, a town which was soon to be caught in a real estate fever and go on a middle-class speculative binge, keyed, as Wolfe lamented, to Yankee materialism and dollar greed. In *You Can't Go Home Again* he described that binge and its painful aftermath in corruscating detail. It would have been hard to find a southern town more thoroughly middle class than Asheville in the years of Wolfe's childhood; yet it was a town still of its region, tasting on its tongue the bitterness of defeat, the sharp sting of southern poverty, and the acrid flavor of racial injustice. This middle-class world was his particular subject throughout his career, although he qualified its customary "booster" optimism by the more pessimistic approach natural to a poverty-stricken region still conscious — as no other part of America is — of defeat.

His mother was Julia Elizabeth Westall Wolfe, a member of a mountain clan memorialized by her son as the "time-devouring" Joyners and Pentlands, and she symbolized for him the protean texture of the South, which was always feminine in his view, "the dark, ruined Helen of his blood." The Westalls were people of some prominence in their region, men and women of medium standing in Asheville and its encircling hills. His mother had been a schoolteacher and a book saleswoman before she became the third wife of William Oliver Wolfe, a native of Pennsylvania. W. O. Wolfe was a stonecutter by profession, owning his own business, and he was a powerful man of great gusto, vast appetites, and a torturing need to assert himself vividly against his drab world. Wolfe's representations of his parents as Eliza and W. O. Gant are among his greatest portraits, and their chance meeting and marriage in a southern hill town were central to his view of the "bitter mystery" of his life. He opens his first novel, *Look Homeward, Angel*, with a speculation on "that dark miracle of chance which makes new magic in a dusty world" and symbolizes it through "A destiny that leads . . . from Epsom into Pennsylvania, and thence into the hills that shut in Altamont." He saw Eugene Gant, the hero of that novel, as "the fusion of two strong egotisms, Eliza's inbrooding and Gant's expanding outward."

Thomas was the youngest of the Wolfe's eight children, of whom three died in infancy. During his childhood his mother bought a boardinghouse and moved into it, taking Thomas and his brother Ben with her and leaving W. O. Wolfe and their daughter Mabel in the old house. (The other two sons were no longer living at home.) Wolfe's childhood was spent in a family divided between two home establishments, with itinerate boarders as his closest companions, except for his brother Ben, whom he idolized and whose death left upon Thomas's spirit a scar that never healed. Wolfe regarded himself in later life as "God's Lonely Man," and he attributed that loneliness to the experiences of his childhood. In 1933 he wrote his sister, "I think I learned about being alone when I was a child about eight years old and I think that I have known about it ever since."

He attended public school until he was eleven; then he entered a small private school operated by Mr. and Mrs. J. M. Roberts. Wolfe was a bright and perceptive boy, and during the four years he spent at the Roberts's school he was almost totally absorbed in learning. At the age of fifteen — three years ahead of his contemporaries — he entered the University of North Carolina at Chapel Hill, the only one of his family to reach that educational level.

At the time he entered it, the university was undergoing the changes that converted it from a leisurely undergraduate liberal arts college into a university engaged in research and graduate instruction and that made it the focal point of the New South movement, the center of southern liberalism. Once more the southern boy was caught up in the fabric of change, confronted by the oppositions of the old and the new. In the university Wolfe proved to be a good student and a "big man on the campus," being active in debate, publications, and fraternities, as well as working with the Playmakers. He was graduated at the age of twenty, with an urge to study further and the desire to become a playwright.

Borrowing from his mother against his anticipated share in his father's estate, Wolfe went to Harvard, where he studied for three years, and earned the Master of Arts degree in English literature. But the central interest of his Harvard years was in the "47 Workshop" in drama and the furtherance of his projected career as a playwright. The picture he paints of the Workshop in *Of Time and the River* is a satiric attack on pretension and lifeless aestheticism, although his portrait of Professor Baker, while tainted with malice, is still drawn with respect.

Teachers as eminent as Professor Lowes praised Wolfe's "very distinct ability," but he vainly tried his fortunes peddling his plays in New York City in the fall of 1923 before he accepted appointment as instructor in English at New York University in January 1924. Wolfe taught at the university, satirically represented as the School of Utility Cultures in *Of Time and the River*, intermittently until the spring of 1930. During this period he made several European tours, met and had a tempestuous love affair with Mrs. Aline Bernstein, a scene and costume designer seventeen years his senior and a married woman with two children. She is the "Esther Jack" of his later novels.

It was in London in the autumn of 1926 that Wolfe began committing to paper in the form of a huge novel the steadily accelerating flood of his childhood memories. The mounting manuscript bore the stamp of the immersion in literature and poetry which had been a major element of Wolfe's life up to that point, but above all, it bore, by his own testimony, the mark of Joyce's *Ulysses*. When he returned to New York, he continued the writing of the book, while his love affair with Mrs. Bernstein waxed and waned and waxed again. Both have left records of the affair, Mrs. Bernstein in *The Journey Down,* an autobiographical novel, and Wolfe in *The Web and the Rock.* How important Mrs. Bernstein was in disciplining Wolfe's monumental flow of memory, energy, and words into the form which *Look Homeward, Angel* had taken by its completion in first draft in March 1928 is a matter of debate but her influence was certainly great. The manuscript of the book was complete, in any case, when, after a violent quarrel with Mrs. Bernstein, Wolfe went again to Europe in July, leaving it with an agent. When he returned to New York in January 1929 it was to find a letter from Maxwell E. Perkins, editor of Charles Scribner's Sons, publishers, expressing an interest in the novel, if it could "be worked into a form publishable by us."

Wolfe renewed the affair with Mrs. Bernstein, to whom *Look Homeward, Angel* is dedicated, and worked desperately to cut and arrange the material of his manuscript into a publishable book. In its original form, *Look Homeward, Angel* was the detailed and intense record of the ancestry, birth, childhood, adolescence, and youth of Eugene Gant. It began with a ninety-page sequence on Eugene's father's life, and it concluded when, after Eugene's graduation from college, he discovers, in an imaginary conversation with the ghost of his brother, that "*You* are your world," and, leaving home, "turns his eyes upon the distant soaring ranges." Perkins insisted on the deletion of the historical opening, on the removal of some extraneous material, and on minor rearrangements, but the novel when it was published on October 18, 1929, probably had undergone little more editorial supervision than long manuscripts by exuberant but talented first novelists generally undergo. As it was to work out, *Look Homeward, Angel* was more unqualifiedly Wolfe's in conception, writing, arrangement, and execution than any other work of long fiction that was ever to be published under his name.

Its lyric intensity and its dramatic power were immediately recognized and hailed; even before Sinclair Lewis, in accepting the Nobel Prize in 1930, praised him highly, Wolfe was recognized as a figure to be reckoned with in the literary world. His native Asheville paid him the tribute of being collectively indignant at the portrait of itself in the novel. A novelistic career of great promise was launched, and Wolfe, who had hungered for fame, suddenly found that he didn't want it. Not only were the members of his family hurt and the people of Asheville angry, but he also felt the obligation of producing a second work that represented an advance over the first. This proved to be one of the major struggles of his life.

He resigned from New York University, ended the affair with Mrs. Bernstein, and went to Europe for a year on a Guggenheim fellowship. When he returned to America, he established himself in an apartment in Brooklyn and took up the lonely vigil with himself and his writing which he describes in *You Can't Go Home Again*. Before *Look Homeward, Angel* was published, he had begun planning the new novel and writing parts of it. During the lonely years in Brooklyn, he struggled in growing desperation to produce the second book. A short novel, *A Portrait of Bascom Hawke*, written to be a part of the book, shared a short novel contest prize of $5,000 offered by *Scribner's Magazine*. Another short novel, *The Web of Earth*, was written and published in *Scribner's Magazine* during the early Brooklyn years. A reminiscence of her life by Eliza Gant, *The Web of Earth* is one of his most successful pieces of work. Nowhere else does the Joycean influence on Wolfe find as direct and as satisfying an expression as it does here.

Wolfe was living on the rather slender proceeds from such sales to magazines of segments of his work. Yet when he was approached by a representative of Metro-Goldwyn-Mayer about the possibility of his doing motion picture writing at $1,000 to $1,500 a week, he declined it on the grounds that he had "a lot of books to write."

He was struggling with a vast novel, to be entitled "The October Fair," which would be in at least four volumes and would have a time span from the Civil War to the present, with hundreds of characters and a new protagonist, David Hawke, replacing Eugene Gant. Maxwell Perkins was working with him every night and on weekends in an attempt to give the new work an acceptable structure and symmetry. It is difficult to separate in Wolfe's letters what is defensible judgment based on fact and what is the frenzied product of his febrile imagination; yet, if his versions are to be trusted even in minor part, Maxwell Perkins had a truly major role to play in the formulation of his second novel. It was Perkins, Wolfe said, who suggested what Wolfe took to be the theme of the new novel, "the search for a father." Seemingly it was Perkins who turned him back to Eugene Gant and away from David Hawke; it was Perkins who discouraged his attempts at formulations of his vision of America in other terms than those of the autobiographical "apprenticeship novel," for Wolfe had worked out a number of elaborate schemes for his new novel. And it was Perkins who insisted that *Of Time and the River* was ready to be published and sent it to the printers despite Wolfe's protest.

Of Time and the River was a mammoth book, continuing the chronicle of Eugene Gant's sensibility. It opens as he leaves Altamont for Harvard, follows him there, to New York City where he teaches in the School of Utility Cultures, to Europe, where he begins the writing of a novel and has a frustrating love affair with a girl named Ann, and concludes as he meets Esther on the boat back to America. *Look Homeward, Angel*, although it had lacked the traditional novelistic structure, had a certain unity through its concentration on a family, a mountain town, and a way of life.

In reading it one was caught up in the sharp impressions of youth and somehow rushed along to that moment of self-realization with which it ended. *Of Time and the River* had less plot, more introspection, less structural cohesion, more rhetoric. Large segments of the book exist without thematic or plot relevance; some of the best scenes and most effective portraits seem to be dramatic intrusions; and it is only when one knows the rest of the story as it is revealed in *The Web and the Rock* that one is able to appreciate the climactic significance of the meeting with Esther with which the book closes.

That these events have meaning for Wolfe beyond their merely personal expression — indeed, that Eugene Gant is in an undefined way the generic Everyman of Whitman's poems or the racial hero of the national epic — one senses from the amount of rhetorical extrapolation by which the hero becomes one with the world, his experiences one with the national experience. Sometimes the rhetoric is wonderfully handled. Indeed, *Of Time and the River* is unusually rich in Wolfe's "poetic passages," but the organization of the materials of the story so that they speak a national myth through self-sufficient action is not attempted with any consistency in the book.

It was greeted with mixed reactions. Many hailed it as a fulfillment of the earnest given by *Look Homeward, Angel*; but its formlessness, its lack of story, and its rhapsodic extravagance were also inescapable, and the really serious critical questions which have been debated about Wolfe's work ever since were first clearly expressed about this novel. These questions are whether it is legitimate in fiction to substitute autobiography and reporting for creation; whether rhetorical assertion, however poetic, can be an acceptable substitute for dramatic representation; whether immediacy can ever be properly bought at the expense of aesthetic distance; and, inevitably, what constitutes form.

In the fall of 1935 a group of stories and sketches originally written as parts of the novel but published in periodicals and excluded from the completed work was assembled and published under the title *From Death to Morning*. This volume, which was attacked by the critics when it appeared and which sold poorly, has never received the attention is deserves. The stories reprinted in it are extremely uneven in quality, but they show Wolfe as a serious experimenter in fiction. His mastery of the short and middle forms of fiction is demonstrated here in such works as "Death the Proud Brother," "Only the Dead Know Brooklyn," "The Four Lost Men," and *The Web of Earth*. That the book would take a critical pounding Wolfe knew, but he said, "I believe that as good writing as I have ever done is in this book." The judgment is startlingly accurate.

Yet if this volume demonstrated a technical virtuosity with which Wolfe is seldom credited, it also showed through its characters and incidents the essential unity and hence the basic autobiographical tendency in his total work. When, in 1936, Wolfe published a little essay in criticism, *The Story of a Novel*, originally a lecture given at a writers' conference at Boulder, Colorado, this record of how he wrote *Of Time and the River*, told with humility and straightforward honesty, seemed to many critics to prove that he simply was not a novelist: in two long novels and a volume of short stories, Wolfe had written out of his direct experience, seemingly without a sense of form, and under the direction of the editors at Scribner's. More than one critic found this situation less than admirable. Robert Penn Warren summed up the case: ". . . despite his admirable energies and his powerful literary endowments, his work illustrates once more the limitations, perhaps the necessary limitations, of an attempt to exploit directly and naïvely the personal experience and the self-defined personality in art." And Bernard De Voto, in a savage attack, declared Wolfe to possess great narrative and dramatic talents but to be unable to realize them in novelistic form; he was guilty of leaving coexisting with true fictional materials too much "placental" matter "which nature and most novelists discard." De Voto also charged that Wolfe's novels were put together by "Mr. Perkins and the assembly-line at Scribner's." That Wolfe was a genius he conceded, but he added that "genius is not enough."

The De Voto article hurt Wolfe deeply. In 1936 a desire to prove De Voto wrong (perhaps heightened by an unconscious awareness that in certain respects at least he was right) joined with many other factors to make Wolfe wish to change his publisher. Among the reasons were a dispute with Perkins about Wolfe's representation of Scribner's people in a story, a disagreement over the cost of corrections in *Of Time and the River*, a group of libel suits which Scribner's wanted to settle out of court, and, most important of all, Wolfe's awareness that his attitudes were incompatible with those of Perkins and that he wanted to go in directions in which Perkins did not wish him to travel. The long and agonizing break with Scribner's, begun in mid 1936, was finally effected in 1937, when Wolfe formed a publishing arrangement with Harper and Brothers, with Edward C. Aswell to act as his editor.

He spent the summer of 1937 working in a cabin in the North Carolina mountains and was happy to find that he was received by his people with pride and pleasure, that they had forgiven him; but he also learned from the experience that "you can't go home again," an idea that loomed large in his thinking and which symbolized for him the fact that we move onward not backward. He was working hard, with the frenzied expenditure of energy of which he was capable, getting material ready to show Aswell as the beginning of a book. At that time he was again projecting a story of great magnitude in at least four volumes, and he was seeking forms and structures through which it could be made into a mythic record of "an innocent man's discovery of life and the world." At one time the book was to be called "The Vision of Spangler's Paul," with the subtitle "The Story of His Birth, His Life, His Going To and Fro in the Earth, His Walking Up and Down in It: His Vision also of the Lost, the Never-Found, the Ever-Here America." At another time he changed his protagonist's name to Doaks, in an effort to symbolize his typical nature, and wrote "The Doaksology," a history of his family. Finally, he selected George Webber as his protagonist — a character physically very much like the David Hawke whom he had wished to make the hero of *Of Time and the River* — and wrote of him: "The protagonist becomes significant not as the tragic victim of circumstances, the romantic hero in conflict and revolt against his environment, but as a kind of polar instrument round which the events of life are grouped, by means of which they are touched, explained, and apprehended, by means of which they are seen and ordered."

In May 1938 he delivered a great mass of manuscript, perhaps a million words, to Aswell. It represented an ordering of the materials on which he was working, but not a book prepared for the press. He himself estimated that more than a year's work remained to be done before the first volume of the new work would be ready. Then he left on a tour of the West which ended with his serious illness from pneumonia in Vancouver, followed by a worsening of his condition in Seattle, and the discovery, after he had been moved to the Johns Hopkins hospital in Baltimore, that the pneumonia had released old sealed-off tuberculosis bacteria in his lungs and that these bacteria had gone to his brain. On September 15, 1938, eighteen days before his thirty-eighth birthday, he died.

Edward Aswell extracted the materials for three books from the mountain of manuscript which Wolfe left. The first, *The Web and the Rock*, is apparently in a form not too different from that which Wolfe had planned, although the last 400 pages of it are still in the earlier and more extravagant style of *Of Time and the River*, rather than the sparser and more controlled style of the opening sections. The new protagonist, George Webber, is surprisingly like Eugene Gant, although his physical characteristics and his family life have changed. The early sections of the book take him through childhood, to college, and then to New York City. There he meets Esther Jack and the novel becomes the record of a tempestuous but passionate love affair. Then Webber goes to Germany, is badly beaten in a riot at a festival, the *Oktoberfest*, in Munich, and, through a monologue between his body and his soul, Webber understands that he must turn from his immersion in himself and his past. "He knew and accepted now its limitations" and ". . . looked calmly and sanely forth upon the earth for the first time in ten years." *The Web and the Rock* is a flawed and very imperfect book, seeming to be the forced union of two inharmonious parts. Yet it is much more nearly a novel than *Of Time and the River*, and in the early parts, prepared for publication during the last year of Wolfe's life, it shows a groping toward the control of material and a desire to represent dramatically rather than to assert rhetorically. Wolfe was still grappling with the problem of novelistic form and language, and grappling with at least limited success.

The second of the books which Aswell assembled is much less a novel than *The Web and the Rock*. *You Can't Go Home Again* is a bringing together in a narrative frame of large units of material which Wolfe had completed but only partially arranged at the time of his death. It continues the story of George Webber, but in it what Wolfe meant when he said that the protagonist was to be a "kind of polar instrument, round which the events of life are grouped," becomes clearer. The book — it is hardly a novel at all — has the very loose narrative structure of George Webber's life: he returns from Europe, writes his book, goes to Lybia Hill (Asheville) for his aunt's funeral, travels in Europe, sees the emptiness of fame in the person of Lloyd McHarg (Sinclair Lewis), travels in Germany and comprehends the horror of the Nazi regime, and writes a long letter setting forth his credo. Yet what gives the book vitality is not George and his experiences — although those dealing with the publication and reception of his novel *Look to the Mountains* are extremely interesting to the Wolfe student — but the view of life which is seen through George. Mr. Katamoto, Mr. Jack and the party at his house, Judge Bland and the satiric picture of the moral and material collapse of Lybia Hill, Daisy Purvis, Lloyd McHarg, Foxhall Edwards and his family, Mr. C. Green, who jumps from the twelfth story of the Admiral Francis Drake Hotel, the frightened little Jew on the train to Paris — it is in such as these that the dramatic strength of the book resides.

You Can't Go Home Again is freer than his other books of the rhapsodic assertion that so often replaces dramatic statement. Those who have found Wolfe's strength in his ability to depict character and to invest scenes with life and movement are likely to find in *You Can't Go Home Again* both his best writing and a discernible promise of greater work and greater control to come. On the other hand, those who see Wolfe's strength to be peculiarly his power with words are likely to feel that the dramatic and narrative success of *You Can't Go Home Again* was bought at the price of his most distinctive qualities. As a novel it is the least satisfactory of his works, yet in its pages are to be seen, dimly and afar off it is true, the faint outline of what he was striving for in his vast and unrealized plans for the "big book."

The third volume that Aswell mined from the manuscript was *The Hills Beyond*, a collection of fragments and sketches. A few of the stories were published in magazines after 1935, but most of them were previously unpublished units of the manuscript. Two distinguished short stories are here, "The Lost Boy," and "Chickamauga," together with a 150-page fragment, "The Hills Beyond," which is a narrative of the Joyners and would have been the early introductory material to the big book. Some of "The Hills Beyond" was originally written as "The Doaksology" and it parallels, in subject matter, material which Wolfe tried to introduce at the beginning of each of his major stories. In this fragment Wolfe's efforts at being an objective novelist have more immediately apparent success than they do elsewhere, and he seems to be moving much more toward the realism of the southern frontier and away from the romanticism of his early career. Valuable though it is to have as many of the self-contained fragments of the Wolfe manuscripts as we can get, *The Hills Beyond* adds very little to Wolfe's stature as a novelist.

In 1948 *Mannerhouse*, one of the plays which Wolfe had tried very hard to peddle to professional producers but without success, was published from the manuscript. It is a document purely of historical importance. With the publication of *The Hills Beyond* in 1941 the corpus of Wolfe's significant work was in print, and, incomplete though it is as a record of his vast and ambitious project, it is all that remains of his efforts to formulate in fiction a vision of himself and his world.

Wolfe's career, like his works, became a matter of debate before his death; and his untimely demise, when seemingly the world was all before him and his prodigious talent was still groping toward an adequate mode of expression, increased the debate without giving appreciable weight to any of the answers. He remains, despite his thirty-seven years, a "golden boy" cut off in the moment of the flowering of his talent, and the issue of whether he had already done all that he was capable of and was, therefore, saved by death from tasting the fruits of a certain diminution of power or whether a major talent went unrealized through the cruel accident of time will remain as unresolved with him as it has been with all the other "golden boys" who tasted too early "the bitter briefness of our days."

The remark of William Faulkner, "I rated Wolfe first [among modern American writers] because we had all failed but Wolfe had made the best failure because he had tried hardest to say the most," is a peculiarly unsatisfying and unrewarding comment which merely restates the question; although his added remark, "He may have had the best talent of us, he may have been 'the greatest American writer' if he had lived longer, though I have never held much with the 'mute inglorious Milton' theory," helps a little.

One of the principal facts of Wolfe's career is summed up in his statement to Edward Aswell, "I began life as a lyrical writer . . . I began to write with an intense and passionate concern with the designs and purposes of my own youth; and like many other men, that preoccupation has now changed to an intense and passionate concern with the designs and purposes of life." This extension of interest to the surrounding world, to "life," was obsessively present with Wolfe from the time of the publication of *Look Homeward, Angel* to his death. In 1929, when the new book was to be "The October Fair," he described it to the Guggenheim Foundation: "It tries to find out why Americans are a nomad race (as this writer believes); why they are touched with a powerful and obscure homesickness wherever they go, both at home and abroad." In 1930 he wrote Perkins: "I believe I am at last beginning to have a proper use of a writer's material: for it seems to me he ought to see in what has happened to him the elements of the universal experience." He wrote John Hall Wheelock, another editor at Scribner's, enthusiastically about a section of "The October Fair" which he had just completed: "In *Antaeus*, in a dozen short scenes, told in their own language, we see people of all sorts *constantly in movement*, going somewhere." But in the same letter he also says, "God knows what Maxwell Perkins will say when he sees it." He was always toying with ideas like his largely unwritten "The Hound of Darkness," of which he said, "It will be a great tone-symphony of night — railway yards, engines, freights, deserts, a clopping hoof, etc. — seen *not by a definite personality*, but haunted throughout by a *consciousness* of personality."

After *Look Homeward, Angel*, he wanted to abandon Eugene Gant for a less autobiographical protagonist, David Hawke, and to write his next novel in the first person — apparently realizing that a first-person narrator is less in the forefront of a story and is more a transmitting vehicle than the third-person protagonist. But during the years of agonized labor by himself and with Perkins most of these plans went by the wayside. Maxwell Perkins believed that Wolfe's second novel should continue the story of Eugene Gant and should center itself exclusively in Gant's consciousness. Perkins wrote, "The principle that I was working on was that this book, too [as *Look Homeward, Angel* had], got its form through the senses of Eugene," and he told how he objected to scenes in the novel that were not recorded through Eugene's perceptions; he tried, for example, to exclude the episodes about Gant's death — one of the most memorable sequences that Wolfe ever wrote. The struggle by which *Of Time and the River* achieved publication over Wolfe's protest is well known; but the depth of Wolfe's dissatisfaction with the book became clear only with the publication of the *Letters* in 1956. When *Of Time and the River* appeared, he wrote Perkins, ". . . as I told you many times, I did not care whether the final length of the book was 300, 500, 1000 pages, so long as I had realized completely and finally my full intention — and that was not realized. I still sweat with anguish —

26

with a sense of irremediable loss — at the thought of what another six months would have done to that book — how much more whole and perfect it would have been. Then there would have been no criticism of its episodic character — for, by God, in purpose and in spirit, that book was not episodic, but a living whole and I could have made it so."

There is certainly the possibility that Wolfe was too completely lost in the deluge of his own memories and words to form them into an intelligent large whole in the years between 1930 and 1935 — although his most distinguished short and middle-length fiction was done in this period — and the sometimes violent midwifery of Perkins may have been essential to getting anything publishable from the laboring author. On the other hand, when one examines the first 300 pages of *The Web and the Rock* and recalls that it is Wolfe's own work done without editorial assistance or thinks of the power and directness of the first two books of *You Can't Go Home Again*, it is difficult not to wish that Wolfe had been free to try.

To the imponderable *if's* which haunt the mind in the case of an artist too youthfully dead must be added in Wolfe's case this one: what might his career have been if he had struggled through toward the realization of form without the assistance of Perkins? Certainly if Wolfe had written *Of Time and the River* without Perkins's aid, it would have been a radically different book and possibly a much better one. The fact remains that only as the lyric recorder of his youth was Wolfe truly successful in the longer fictional forms. His great vision of being the critic of his society and the definer of his nation can be seen in fragments but its large outline is shadowy and incomplete.

It is for this reason that the central problems concerning Wolfe as a writer are as intimately tied up in his personality and his career as they are in his work. Louis D. Rubin, Jr., in an excellent critical study of Wolfe, has asked that the autobiographical quality of the novels be accepted as clear fact and they then be examined as novels, as works of art. When this is done — and Mr. Rubin does it with great skill — *Look Homeward, Angel* emerges as Wolfe's only satisfactory book and in the rest of his work one almost has the feeling of an expense of talent in a waste of formlessness. Perhaps such a conclusion is proper — certainly it is the one reached by many of the best and most rigorous of American critics — but it leaves untouched the question of Wolfe's power and the continuing and mounting success which he has with readers.

Wolfe's failure to write his own books as he wanted them written cannot ultimately be laid at any door other than his own. The causes of this failure are complex: they include his own lack of security, and his extreme sensitivity to reviews shows that such a lack was there; his desire to achieve publication at whatever cost, and there is evidence of this quality in his letters; and a deep-seated affection for Perkins and gratitude to him. As William Faulkner once declared, "The writer's only responsibility is to his art. He will be completely ruthless if he is a good one . . . If a writer has to rob his mother, he will not hesitate." Paradoxically, Thomas Wolfe devoted his life and his energies to the creation of art with a single-mindedness not surpassed in this century — he is almost archetypally the "dedicated writer" — and yet he lacked that ultimate ruthlessness of which Faulkner speaks. For a writer whose talent is of the magnitude of Wolfe's and whose plans have the scope and importance that his do, such a failing cannot be easily brushed aside. On this point he was highly culpable — he did not make the longer forms of fiction, at whatever cost, the adequate vehicles of his vision and his talent; he did not subject his ego to the discipline of his own creative imagination — and the price he has paid for the failure has been very great indeed. It is the price of being a writer of inspired fragments and of only one satisfying larger work and that an imperfect one.

Here the oppositions in Wolfe reach a crucial test. He seemed always to feel that when the contrasting opposites were defined the synthesis would result automatically; he was always stating a thing and its opposite and allowing the "miracle" of their coexistence to stand. Here in his own work the fact of his great talent and the fact of his ambitious projects were never submitted to the discipline which would have made a synthesis of them; they were allowed to coexist without serious efforts at fusion.

This aspect of Wolfe's work points to its essential romanticism, to the extent to which it is imbedded in the doctrine of self-expression and self-realization. Whitman once wrote: " 'Leaves of Grass' . . . has mainly been the outcropping of my own emotional and other personal nature — an attempt, from first to last, to put a *Person* . . . freely, fully and truly on record." This is basically Wolfe's accomplishment, although he was clearly striving toward something else in the last seven years of his life.

Wolfe's work is not, therefore, of primary value as a group of novels, or even in terms of his shadowy larger plan. His total work stands, like so many monuments of romantic art, a group of fragments imperfectly bodying forth a seemingly ineffable cosmic vision in terms of the self of the artist. Although it contains large areas of poor and even bad writing, scenes that do not come off or that bear no relevance to what has gone before, and rhapsodies that fail utterly to communicate, it also contains some of the best writing done by an American this century, and its merits our thoughtful examination.

The most obvious of Wolfe's strengths is his ability with language. The word has for him unique powers; he was fascinated by language, enchanted with rhythms and cadences, enamored of rhetorical devices. Language was the key he sought to unlock mysteries and to unloose vast forces; he approached it almost in the spirit of primitive magic. This aspect of language he expressed in the paragraph printed as a prologue to *The Web and the Rock*: "Could I make tongue say more than tongue could utter! Could I make brain grasp more than brain could think! Could I weave into immortal denseness some small brede of words, pluck out of sunken depths the roots of living, some hundred thousand magic words that were as great as all my hunger, and hurl the sum of all my living out upon three hundred pages — then death could take my life, for I had lived it ere he took it: I had slain hunger, beaten death!"

Another aspect of his effective use of language is his accurate and vivid dialogue. Wolfe had a remarkable ear for folk speech, and his people speak personal dialects set down with great verisimilitude. His characters sometimes seem to talk forever, but their speech is always marked by distinctiveness in diction, syntax, and cadence. Accuracy, however, is a less obvious quality of their speech than gusto and vigor are. There is a feeling of great energy in the speech of most of them. The clearest example of Wolfe's mastery of the spoken language is to be seen in *The Web of Earth* but it is apparent in almost everything that he wrote.

He sought, he declared, a language, an articulation: "I believe with all my heart, also, that each man for himself and in his own way, each man who ever hopes to make a living thing out of the substances of his one life, must find that way, that language, and that door — must find it for himself." He sought this language, this tool of communication, not only in the rolling periods of rhetoric but also in the sensuous image drawn from the "world's body," which is a distinctive aspect of the language of lyric and dramatic writing. And here, in the concrete and particularized representation of the sensory world, he was triumphantly the master. It is Wolfe's ability to evoke the world's body which is responsible for the sense of total reality which his work produces in the young and impressionable, and it is this seeming immersion in the sensuous which makes him sometimes appear to be more the poet of the senses than of sense.

This concern with language, one so great that he might have said of his total work, as Whitman did of *Leaves of Grass*, that it was "only a language experiment," is the logical expression of one of Wolfe's major themes, the loneliness at the core of all human experience. He saw each individual in the world as living in a compartment in isolation from his fellows and unable to communicate adequately with them. It is this tragedy of loneliness that is at the heart of Eugene Gant's experience and makes *Look Homeward, Angel* a book which can appropriately bear the subtitle "A Story of the Buried Life." The desire to break down the walls keeping him from communion with others is at least a part of "man's hunger in his youth," in *Of Time and the River*. The need Wolfe's characters have for a language with which to breach the isolating walls is very great. In a scene in *Of Time and the River*, Helen, Eugene Gant's sister, is lying awake in the darkness: "And suddenly, with a feeling of terrible revelation, she saw the strangeness and mystery of man's life; she felt about her in the darkness the presence of ten thousand people, each lying in his bed, naked and alone, united at the heart of night and darkness, and listening, as she, to the sounds of silence and of sleep. . . . And it seemed to her that if men would only listen in the darkness, and send the language of their naked lonely spirits across the silence of the night, all of the error, falseness and confusion of their lives would vanish, they would no longer be strangers, and each would find the life he sought and never yet had found." There are few lonelier people in fiction than W. O. and Eliza Gant. Each is lost in an envelope of private experience and each tries vainly to express himself — W. O. through rhetoric, invective, alcohol, and lust; Eliza through garrulity, money, and real estate. The terrible incompatibility in which they live reaches its almost shocking climax when, in the last moments of Gant's life, they finally speak across the void to each other, and Gant's expression of kindness dissolves Eliza into tears.

Wolfe described the controlling theme of all his books as "the search for a father" — the theme he said he consciously made central in *Of Time and the River* at Perkins's suggestion. But he defined that search as a search for certainty, an "image of strength and wisdom external to his [man's] need and superior to his hunger." In one sense, this search is the seeking for an individual with whom communication can be established and maintained. The search grows out of Eugene's loneliness in his childhood and the sense of isolation which he has in his world. It is intensified by his inability to communicate his love to his brother Ben. In his later life, whether for Gant or for George Webber, it finds expression in the relations established and broken with Francis Starwick, Esther Jack, and Foxhall Edwards, to name only the major figures. About all these relationships there is a recurrent pattern: the new person is approached with eagerness; an intense relationship is established; then a failure of communication and understanding occurs; and Gant-Webber rejects the friendship. The affair with Esther Jack is, perhaps, the clearest example of this pattern. It is debatable whether the idea of the search for the father, with its suggestion of myth and of fable, defines as well as does the representation of loneliness the fundamental theme of Thomas Wolfe, whether that loneliness be described as the search for "a stone, a leaf, an unfound door," as the urge to wandering and the counter tug of home (so well articulated in *The Web of Earth* and parts of *Of Time and the River*), or as the desire vicariously to be one with and to understand "ten thousand men" in the cities, the towns, and the hamlets of America.

Here Wolfe's concern with oppositions takes on its tragic overtone. The essentially contradictory aspect of life creates barriers of race, of place, of heritage, of language, and each of us can say with Wolfe at the end of the Gant-Webber chronicle, as he says at its beginning: "Naked and alone we came into exile. In her dark womb we did not know our mother's face: from the prison of her flesh have we come into the unspeakable and incommunicable prison of this earth." Thus, as Wolfe sees it, all human experience seeks the "great forgotten language, the lost lane-end into heaven." Certainly, as several critics have pointed out, there are Wordsworthian suggestions here. Out of some transcendent glory of childhood, we gradually are hemmed in by the growing prison house of the world, the luster and glory of life are gradually tarnished, and we are forced further away from communion. But there are also suggestions of a book which Wolfe knew and praised and whose formlessness he defended, Laurence Sterne's *Tristram Shandy*. Sterne's novel is concerned with the education of the young through the impact of the world outside upon the young mind. It is told through the memories in maturity of Tristram, and it is the associational pattern of those memories which determines the form of the book. At the core of *Tristram Shandy* is the tragedy of isolation. W. O. Gant has in one sense a recognizable ancestor in "My Father" Walter Shandy, who sought in vain for a word to communicate with wife and brother. Loneliness, memory, and time are intertwined in the sad comedy of the Shandean world. And so they are in Wolfe's.

For while the Wolfean character cannot find a language through which to speak, cannot break through "the incommunicable prison of this earth," he is the victim of more than silence and the lack of a language — he is also the victim of time. And the entity time is for Wolfe the great factor in life and in his books, and the only really serious philosophical concept which he uses in his fiction. One of the structural problems with which he grappled seriously through his novelistic career was finding a means of representing adequately his views of time, which he saw as threefold.

The first and most obvious element of time, he believed, is that of simple chronology, the element that carries a narrative forward; this may be called "clock time." The second element is past time, the "accumulated impact of man's experience so that each moment of their lives was conditioned not only by what they experienced in that moment, but by all that they had experienced up to that moment." This past time exists in the present principally through the action of the memory, being triggered by a concrete sensory impression which in some way recalls the past. However, as Margaret Church has pointed out, memory in Wolfe merely recalls this past; it does not re-create it or actually assert its continued existence, as Bergson's and Proust's theories of time tend to do. All this action — the present and the recollections of the past in the present — takes place against what Wolfe calls "time immutable, the time of rivers, mountains, oceans, and the earth; a kind of eternal and unchanging universe of time against which would be projected the transience of man's life, the bitter briefness of his day." It is this inexorable forward flow of time, pictured as a river or more often as a train, which constantly carries man away from his golden youth, which is "lost and far" and can exist again only in memory.

Wolfe's problem was the picturing of scenes so that an awareness of these three elements of time was created. In a given situation a man caught in his particular instant in time has it enriched and rendered more meaningful as the past impinges upon him through memory, and he gets thereby a sense of the absolute time within which his days are painfully brief. Wolfe gives this concept fictional expression in his four-part story "The Lost Boy." In the first part, a boy, Grover, passes an initiation point in life, as his father intercedes for him with a candy store keeper. " 'This is Time,' thought Grover. 'Here is the Square, here is my father's shop, and here am I.' " The second part is the mother's reminiscence years later about Grover on a train trip to the St. Louis fair. Her monologue ends, "It was so long ago, but when I think of it, it all comes back . . . I can still see Grover just the way he was, the way he looked that morning when we went down through Indiana, by the river, to the Fair." The third part is a monologue by the sister, recounting Grover's death. It ends, "It all comes back as if it happened yesterday. And then it goes away again, and seems farther off and stranger than if it happened in a dream." In the fourth part, the brother, who was a very small boy when Grover died, goes to the house in St. Louis where it happened and tries by the use of memory to bring back the "lost boy." This section ends: "And out of the enchanted wood, that thicket of man's memory, Eugene knew that the dark eye and the quiet face of his friend and brother — poor child, life's stranger, and life's exile, lost like all of us, a cipher in blind mazes, long ago — the lost boy was gone forever, and would not return." The ultimate meaning of the statement "You can't go home again," which Wolfe used over and over in the last year of his life, is to be found here. "Home" is a symbol of the past, of what has been lost; for the holder of a romantic view of childhood, it is a peculiarly effective and revealing symbol. None of us, it says, can return to the lost childhood, the lost community, the fading glory; for time carries us inexorably away. We can't go home again.

In Wolfe's work this vision of time is always associated with the sense of being alone, of being isolated. In *Of Time and the River* he tries to enumerate the concrete memories which taken together make up the remembered past for America, and then he says: "But this was the reason why these things could never be forgotten — because we are so lost, so naked and so lonely in America.

Immense and cruel skies bend over us, and all of us are driven on forever and we have no home. Therefore, it is not the slow, the punctual sanded drip of the unnumbered days that we remember best, the ash of time; nor is it the huge monotone of the lost years, the unswerving schedules of the lost life and the well-known faces, that we remember best. It is a face seen once and lost forever in a crowd, an eye that looked, a face that smiled and vanished on a passing train." And a little later, he describes the way in which the past almost forcefully entered the present for him: ". . . always when that lost world would come back, it came at once, like a sword thrust through the entrails, in all its panoply of past time, living, whole, and magic as it had always been." It is like a sword because it cuts sharply and deeply and hurts very much. Perhaps the one emotion which Wolfe describes most effectively is this pain from which comes the sudden hunger for a lost and almost forgotten aspect of life, for "the apple tree, the singing, and the gold." Wolfe succeeds in giving us this sense of the onward rush of time and the death of the morning's gold, an awareness of the price that is paid before the "years of philosophic calm" can come. Since this feeling is very much a part of youth and its pain and *weltschmerz*, its inarticulate melancholy, he speaks with peculiar authority to the very young and to those older chiefly through their memories of having been very young.

Wolfe did not theorize about these concepts of time, or, except in passing, discuss them. He probably did not know the works of Proust at all well, despite the degree to which the sense impressions in the present restored the lost past for both of them. Karin Pfister has suggested that Wolfe's time theories may owe something to those of Bergson, to whom Proust was also a debtor. As a novelist Wolfe seemingly was fascinated by the mystery rather than the metaphysics of time. In *The Web and the Rock* he wrote: "Time is a fable and a mystery . . . it broods over all the images of earth . . . Time is collected in great clocks and hung in towers . . . and each man has his own, a different time."

The river and the ocean he used as large symbols for "time immutable," yet his clearest figure for the ceaseless motion and the inexorable passage of time is the train. No American in the past fifty years has been more the poet of trains. Their rushing across the face of the earth, the glimpses of life to be seen flashing past their speeding windows, the nostalgic and lonely wail of their whistles in the night, even their sounds echoing in depots, which in *Of Time and the River* he imagines to be the very sounds of time itself — all these characteristics Wolfe associates with loneliness and movement and the sad passage of time.

Yet in one sense Wolfe's characters transcend his themes. The paradox here is a very great one : Wolfe, who asserted that no man could know his brother, described his fellowmen with deep understanding; Wolfe, whose subject seemed always to be himself, whose characters are drawn in large measure from real life rather than imagined, and who presented his world chiefly through the consciousness of an autobiographical hero, created a group of characters so fully realized that they live with great vigor in the reader's mind. *Look Homeward, Angel* is perhaps the most autobiographical novel ever written by an American, yet the protagonist, Eugene Gant, is a much less vivid person than the members of his family. It is W. O. Gant, Eliza, Helen, and brother Ben who glow with life and absorb our imaginations. Eugene himself is more a communicating vehicle than a person, or perhaps it is that he seems to us more nearly ourselves and less someone whom we are observing. In *Of Time and the River* the Gant family, Bascom Pentland, Francis Starwick, Abraham Jones, and Ann are more convincingly persons than the hero is. In *The Web and the Rock*, there is less centering in the consciousness of the protagonist and George Webber exists more as an individual than Eugene does.

The result is that the other characters of this novel and *You Can't Go Home Again* are seen in relation to the protagonist rather than through him. Yet in these books too Wolfe's gift for creating believable people of unbelievable gusto is very impressive. Certainly among all his memorable creations Esther Jack, Dick Prosser, Nebraska Crane, Judge Rumford Bland, and Foxhall Edwards would stand high.

Wolfe's concentration upon people of excessive vigor may be the result of his vitalism, his worship of life as a pervasive force and a supreme value in itself. Certainly, whether as the result of philosophical attitude or of mere artistic excess, the characters in Wolfe's work loom larger than life and are possessed of an awesome and sometimes awful dynamism. They are large in body, appetite, feeling, disease, and suffering. They crowd the canvas to the exclusion of the background and even of the context of action. Possibly this lack of aesthetic distance, which is one of the most obvious qualities of Wolfe's work, results from his extreme subjectivity, but it is also attributable in part to his view of life. Bella Kussy thinks that the example of vitalism run rampant which Wolfe saw in Nazi Germany cured him, and that the German experience caused his concern in his last years with social rather than personal consequences. The tendency toward social criticism, however, was present in his work some time before he was made shockingly aware of the direction that Nazi Germany was taking.

Among the important influences on the social aspect of Wolfe's work was that of Sinclair Lewis, whose satiric condemnation of a materialistic society dedicated to bulk, glitter, and the conscious disregard of beauty made a powerful impact on the young writer. As early as 1923 Wolfe wrote his mother contemptuously of "those people who shout 'Progress, Progress, Progress' — when what they mean is more Ford automobiles, more Rotary Clubs, more Baptist Ladies Social unions." This attitude is just about the extent of the social criticism in *Look Homeward, Angel*, although it is often expressed in that novel. Wolfe's tendency toward satire is clearly present in the book, but it is satire aimed at Main Street and Booster's Club targets; in the name of beauty it is attacking blatant commercialism and its attendant ugliness.

The years that Wolfe spent in Brooklyn during the depths of the depression were filled with social lessons for him. "Everywhere around me," he wrote later, "during these years, I saw the evidence of an incalculable ruin and suffering. . . . universal calamity had somehow struck the life of almost every one I knew." He became convinced that something was basically wrong with such a social order. His letters show that he had wanted to make what he and Perkins regarded as a "Marxist" interpretation of the social scene in *Of Time and the River*, although Perkins dissuaded him from doing it. The egalitarianism and the essentially middle-class economic radicalism of his native region reasserted themselves in his thinking during this period, and in *You Can't Go Home Again* they find expression. A sense of primary social injustice in the world is an operative force in Book II, "The World That Jack Built," which contrasts the world of the very wealthy with that of the laboring classes that serve it; in the section "The Hollow Men," dealing with the suicide of C. Green and asserting the primary worth of the individual in a society that would reduce him to a mere statistic; in Book IV, " 'I Have a Thing to Tell You,' " with its angry picture of Nazi Germany; and in the satiric pictures of Lybia Hill in the grip of the real estate boom and in the disaster of the crash, where ignoble motives of little men play destructively upon the common greed of their fellow citizens.

One of the repeated charges that Wolfe made against Perkins was that he was a "conservative," whereas Wolfe had become what he called a "revolutionary." Yet his social thinking is lacking in depth and significance. Pamela H. Johnson is probably too harsh when she says, "His is a young man's socialism, based on the generous rage, the infuriated baffled pity; like the majority of young, middle-class intellectuals, he looked for 'the people' in the doss-house and upon the benches of the midnight parks." But, as E. B. Burgum has noted, ". . . he was so constituted that he must fight alone." In that aloneness he was unable to act as a part of any coordinated social scheme. The future of America which he asserts at the conclusion of *You Can't Go Home Again* is really an act of faith — and of a faith still based on the spirit as opposed to the material, on the reawakening of "our own democracy" within us. Here, as social critic, he reminds us most of Whitman again. For Whitman in *Democratic Vistas* saw with mounting alarm the pattern that his nation was following and opposed it to the expanding realization of the self, of "Personalism," which it was the poet's program to advance. This is a defensible and even an admirable position, but the work of those who hold it can seldom bear the logical scrutiny of those who espouse specific social programs. As contrasted with Maxwell Perkins, Wolfe properly regarded himself as a "revolutionary," yet he remained the most persuasive advocate of an enlightened middle-class democracy that America has produced this century.

It was inevitable that the centrality of loneliness and separateness in Wolfe's experience and his writing, coupled with the social problems and the human suffering of the years of his active career, should have fostered in him a sense of evil in the world and have given a tragic quality to his writing. His very method of oppositions would lead him to a Manichaean cosmic view. Furthermore, he was a product of a region steeped in defeat, suffering, and the acceptance of an unthinkable inevitability. As C. Vann Woodward has stated it, "Nothing about [its] history is conducive to the theory that the South was the darling of divine providence." Something of this attitude — which, in Wolfe,.E. B. Burgum inaccurately called "reconciliation with despair" — is a part of the heritage of all southerners, even in the liberal areas of the South such as the one in which Wolfe grew up.

Wolfe wrote of the shock he experienced in Brooklyn during the depression at the "black picture of man's inhumanity to his fellow man . . . of suffering, violence, oppression, hunger, cold, and filth and poverty," and added, "And from it all, there has come the final deposit, a burning memory, a certain evidence of the fortitude of man, his ability to suffer and somehow to survive." Loneliness and suffering and pain and death — these are the things which man — frail, weak, hauntingly mortal — can expect. Yet man, for Wolfe, is also a noble creature. The despair of the literary naturalist, so common in America in the twentieth century, is not a part of his thinking. In a too obvious extension of a speech by Hamlet in the twenty-seventh chapter of *You Can't Go Home Again*, Wolfe attempts to answer the question "What is man?" and in his answer states as clearly as he was ever to do the basic contradiction and the tragic magnitude of the earthly experience. Man is "a foul, wretched, abominable creature . . . it is impossible to say the worst of him . . . this travesty of waste and sterile breath." Yet his accomplishments are magnificent. The individual, viewed as physical animal, is a "frail and petty thing who lives his days and dies like all the other animals and is forgotten. And yet, he is immortal, too, for both the good and the evil that he does live after him." In the teeming, uneven pages of Wolfe's work this vision of man possessed of tragic grandeur — essentially the vision of the nineteenth-century Romantic — is presented with great intensity.

Wolfe believed that the American experience demanded a new art form and a new language for the expression of this view, however. Like Whitman, he invited the Muse to "migrate from Greece and Ionia," and

> Making directly for this rendezvous, vigorously clearing
> a path for herself, striding through the confusion,
> By thud of machinery and shrill steam-whistle
> undismay'd,
> Bluff'd not a bit by drain-pipe, gasometers, artificial
> fertilizers,
> Smiling and pleas'd with palpable intent to stay,
> She's here, install'd amid the kitchen ware!

Wolfe wrote: ". . . in the cultures of Europe and of the Orient the American artist can find no antecedent scheme, no structural plan, no body of tradition that can give his own work the validity and truth that it must have. It is not merely that he must make somehow a new tradition for himself, derived from his own life and from the enormous space and energy of American life . . . it is even more than this, that the labor of a complete and whole articulation, the discovery of an entire universe and of a complete language, is the task that lies before him."

In his attempt to accomplish that task Wolfe strove with unceasing diligence. That he failed to realize the full structural plan of his work in the years in which he lived is obvious; that he made no whole articulation of the space and energy of American life is obvious; that he failed to formulate a completely adequate language for the singer of America in fiction is also obvious. What he might have done and even why he did not accomplish more of it become finally unanswerable questions; they tease the mind without enlightening it. We must ultimately accept or reject what he did accomplish. That work—however flawed, imperfect, fragmentary—is ultimately the record of a self and only very partially that of a nation. Wolfe himself described its strength and suggested its great weakness when he called it "a giant web in which I was caught, the product of my huge inheritance — the torrential recollectiveness, derived out of my mother's stock, which became a living, million-fibered integument that bound me to the past, not only of my own life, but of the very earth from which I came, so that nothing in the end escaped from its inrooted and all-feeling explorativeness." To the end Thomas Wolfe retained a childlike, pristine delight in the manifold shapes, colors, odors, sounds, and textures of experience and his work communicates this delight — shadowed with a nostalgia for things past — with almost total authority.

The measure of this accomplishment is not small. *Look Homeward, Angel* is a richly evocative account of the pains and joys of childhood and youth, peopled with a host of living characters. With all its flaws, it is a fine novel, and one that gives promise of enduring. In Wolfe's total work a personality is set down with a thoroughness and an honesty, with an intensity and a beauty of language unsurpassed by any other American prose writer, even though, aside from *Look Homeward, Angel*, it is only in the short novels that we find really sure artistic control, and sprinkled through the other books are passages of very bad writing and of irrelevant action.

Wolfe began obsessed with paradox and contradiction; the shape of his whole career reflects startling contrast. He who would have written the definition of his nation left primarily the definition of a self; he who would have asserted that though we "are lost here in America . . . we shall be found" was from birth to death a lonely man, vainly seeking communion. He survives — and probably will continue to survive — as the chronicler of a lost childhood, a vanished glory, the portrayer of an individual American outlined, stark and lonely, beneath a cruel sky.

⤴ Selected Bibliography

Principal Works of Thomas Wolfe

Look Homeward, Angel. New York: Scribner's, 1929.
Of Time and the River. New York: Scribner's, 1935.
From Death to Morning. New York: Scribner's, 1935.
The Story of a Novel. New York: Scribner's, 1936.
The Web and the Rock. New York: Harper, 1939.
You Can't Go Home Again. New York: Harper, 1940.
The Hills Beyond. New York: Harper, 1943.
Thomas Wolfe's Letters to His Mother Julia Elizabeth Wolfe, edited with an Introduction by John Skally Terry. New York: Scribner's, 1943.
Mannerhouse: A Play in a Prologue and Three Acts. New York: Harper, 1948.
A Western Journal. Pittsburgh: University of Pittsburgh Press, 1951.
The Correspondence of Thomas Wolfe and Homer Andrew Watt, edited by Oscar Cargill and Thomas Clark Pollock. New York: New York University Press, 1954.
The Letters of Thomas Wolfe, collected and edited by Elizabeth Nowell. New York: Scribner's, 1956.
"Welcome to Our City: A 10-Scene Play," *Esquire Magazine*, 48:58–83 (October 1957).

Books of Selections from the Writings of Thomas Wolfe

The Face of a Nation: Poetical Passages from the Writings of Thomas Wolfe [selected by John Hall Wheelock]. New York: Scribner's, 1939.
A Stone, A Leaf, A Door: Poems by Thomas Wolfe, selected and arranged in verse by John S. Barnes. New York: Scribner's, 1945.
The Portable Thomas Wolfe, edited by Maxwell Geismar. New York: Viking, 1946. (Contains *The Story of a Novel*, episodes from each of the novels, and six short stories.)

Current American Reprints

The Hills Beyond. New York: Pyramid Books. $.50.
Look Homeward, Angel. New York: Modern Library Giant (Random House). $2.95. New York: Scribner Library. $1.95.
The Web and the Rock. New York: Universal Library (Grosset and Dunlap). $1.45. New York: Harper's Modern Classics. $1.80.

44

You Can't Go Home Again. New York: Universal Library. $1.45. New York: Harper's Modern Classics. $1.80.

Bibliographies

Holman, C. Hugh. "Thomas Wolfe: A Bibliographical Study," *Texas Studies in Literature and Language,* 1:427–45 (Autumn 1959).

Johnson, Elmer D. *Of Time and Thomas Wolfe: A Bibliography with a Character Index of His Works.* New York: Scarecrow Press, 1959.

Kauffman, Bernice. "Bibliography of Periodical Articles on Thomas Wolfe," *Bulletin of Bibliography,* 17:162–65, 172–90 (May, August 1942).

Preston, George R., Jr. *Thomas Wolfe: A Bibliography.* New York: Charles S. Boesen, 1943.

Critical and Biographical Studies

Adams, Agatha Boyd. *Thomas Wolfe: Carolina Student.* Chapel Hill: University of North Carolina Library, 1950.

Beach, Joseph Warren. *American Fiction: 1920–1940.* New York: Macmillan, 1941. Pp. 173–215.

Delakas, Daniel L. *Thomas Wolfe, la France, et les romanciers français.* Paris: Jouve & Cie., 1950.

Geismar, Maxwell. *Writers in Crisis.* Boston: Houghton Mifflin, 1942. Pp. 185–236.

Johnson, Pamela Hansford. *Hungry Gulliver.* New York: Scribner's, 1948. (An American edition of *Thomas Wolfe: A Critical Study.* London: William Heinemann, 1947.)

Muller, Herbert J. *Thomas Wolfe.* Norfolk, Conn.: New Directions, 1947.

Norwood, Hayden. *The Marble Man's Wife: Thomas Wolfe's Mother.* New York: Scribner's, 1947.

Pfister, Karin. *Zeit und Wirklichkeit bei Thomas Wolfe.* Heidelberg: Carl Winter, 1954.

Pollock, Thomas Clark, and Oscar Cargill. *Thomas Wolfe at Washington Square.* New York: New York University Press, 1954.

Reeves, George M., Jr. *Thomas Wolfe et Europe.* Paris: Librarie Marcel Didier, 1955.

Rubin, Louis D., Jr. *Thomas Wolfe: The Weather of His Youth.* Baton Rouge: Louisiana State University Press, 1955.

Walser, Richard, ed. *The Enigma of Thomas Wolfe: Biographical and Critical Selections.* Cambridge, Mass.: Harvard University Press, 1953.

Watkins, Floyd C. *Thomas Wolfe's Characters: Portraits from Life.* Norman: University of Oklahoma Press, 1957.

Articles

*Albrecht, W. P. "Time as Unity in Thomas Wolfe," *New Mexico Quarterly Review*, 19:320–29 (Autumn 1949).

Baker, Carlos. "Thomas Wolfe's Apprenticeship," *Delphian Quarterly*, 23:20–25 (January 1940).

Bishop, John Peale. "The Sorrows of Thomas Wolfe," *Kenyon Review*, 1:7–17, (Winter 1939).

*Brown, E. K. "Thomas Wolfe: Realist and Symbolist," *University of Toronto Quarterly*, 10:153–66 (January 1941).

*Burgum, Edwin B. "Thomas Wolfe's Discovery of America," *Virginia Quarterly Review*, 22:421–37 (Summer 1946).

*Church, Margaret. "Thomas Wolfe: Dark Time," *PMLA*, 64:629–38 (September 1949).

*Collins, Thomas L. "Thomas Wolfe," *Sewanee Review*, 50:487–504 (October–December 1942).

Cowley, Malcolm. "Thomas Wolfe," *Atlantic Monthly*, 200:202–12 (November 1957).

*De Voto, Bernard. "Genius Is Not Enough," *Saturday Review of Literature*, 13:3–4, 14–15 (April 25, 1936).

*Frohock, W. M. "Thomas Wolfe: Of Time and Neurosis," *Southwest Review*, 33:349–60 (Autumn 1948).

Geismar, Maxwell. "Thomas Wolfe: The Hillman and the Furies," *Yale Review*, 35:649–66 (Summer 1946).

Holman, C. Hugh. "The Loneliness at the Core," *New Republic*, 133:16–17 (October 10, 1955).

Kennedy, William F. "Economic Ideas in Contemporary Literature — The Novels of Thomas Wolfe," *Southern Economic Journal*, 20:35–50 (July 1953).

Kussy, Bella. "The Vitalist Trend and Thomas Wolfe," *Sewanee Review*, 50:306–23 (July–September 1942).

Ledig-Rowohlt, H. M. "Thomas Wolfe in Berlin," *American Scholar*, 22:185–201 (Spring 1953).

Little, Thomas. "The Thomas Wolfe Collection of William B. Wisdom," *Harvard Library Bulletin*, 1:280–87 (Autumn 1947).

McElderry, B. R., Jr. "The Autobiographical Problem in Thomas Wolfe's Earlier Novels," *Arizona Quarterly*, 4:315–24 (Winter 1948).

———. "The Durable Humor of *Look Homeward, Angel*," *Arizona Quarterly*, 11:123–28 (Summer 1955).

Natanson, Maurice. "The Privileged Moment: A Study in the Rhetoric of Thomas Wolfe," *Quarterly Journal of Speech*, 43:143–50 (April 1957).

*Articles preceded by an asterisk are in Walser, *The Enigma of Thomas Wolfe.*

Perkins, Maxwell. "Thomas Wolfe," *Harvard Library Bulletin*, 1:269–77 (Autumn 1947).

Ribalow, Harold U. "Of Jews and Thomas Wolfe," *Chicago Jewish Forum*, 13:89–99 (1954).

*Rothman, Nathan L. "Thomas Wolfe and James Joyce: A Study in Literary Influence," *Southern Vanguard*, edited by Allen Tate. New York: Prentice-Hall, 1947. Pp. 52–77.

Simpson, Claude M., Jr. "Thomas Wolfe: A Chapter in His Biography," *Southwest Review*, 25:308–21 (April 1940).

*Stearns, Monroe M. "The Metaphysics of Thomas Wolfe," *College English*, 6:193–99 (January 1945).

Taylor, Walter Fuller. "Thomas Wolfe and the Middle-Class Tradition," *South Atlantic Quarterly*, 52:543–54 (October 1953).

*Thompson, Betty. "Thomas Wolfe: Two Decades of Criticism," *South Atlantic Quarterly*, 49:378–92 (July 1950).

*Volkening, Henry T. "Thomas Wolfe: Penance No More," *Virginia Quarterly Review*, 5:196–215 (Spring 1939).

*Warren, Robert Penn. "A Note on the Hamlet of Thomas Wolfe," *American Review*, 5:191–208 (May 1935).

Watkins, Floyd C. "Thomas Wolfe and the Nashville Agrarians," *Georgia Review*, 7:410–23 (Winter 1953).

———. "Thomas Wolfe and the Southern Mountaineer," *South Atlantic Quarterly*, 50:58–71 (January 1951).